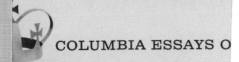

COLUMBIA ESSAYS O

W

NUMBER 8

PRICE $1.00

C. P. SNOW

by Robert Gorham Davis

C. P. Snow

by ROBERT GORHAM DAVIS

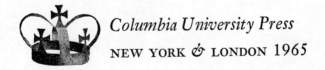

Columbia University Press
NEW YORK & LONDON 1965

COLUMBIA ESSAYS ON MODERN WRITERS is a series of critical studies of English, Continental, and other writers whose works are of contemporary artistic and intellectual significance.

Editor: William York Tindall

Advisory Editors

Jacques Barzun   W.T.H. Jackson   Joseph A. Mazzeo   Justin O'Brien

C. P. Snow is Number 8 of the series.

ROBERT GORHAM DAVIS is Professor of English at Columbia University. The editor of *Ten Modern Masters,* Professor Davis is widely known for his book reviews, which appear in the nation's leading media.

C. P. Snow

Since his influential Rede Lecture, "The Two Cultures," in 1958, it has seemed deceptively easy to place Charles Percy Snow—both as novelist and man of ideas. In that lecture and any number of public appearances, he has done the placing for us. We think that we know, through Snow himself, precisely where he stands and what he wants.

The most powerful revolutionary force in the world today, his lecture told us, is science—science lifted to a new level by Einstein, Rutherford, Kapitza, Bohr, and Dirac. Its heroic age was the 1920s; the center of activity was Cambridge, where Snow himself, then a research student, heard these men describe their discoveries as they were making them.

Science is essentially progressive, Snow argues, and so are the political views of most of its creators. They possess the means—and the desire—to end want and disease in every corner of the world. They see no necessary barriers to collaboration with their colleagues in the Communist countries. Ultimately, of course, scientists have to face as individuals the facts of the human condition, face loneliness and death. Their interest in literature, unfortunately, tends to be minimal.

Literary men, on the other hand, according to Snow, have little or no knowledge of the new science, and their social attitudes are often contemptible. A physicist of distinction said to him: "Yeats, Pound, Wyndham Lewis, nine out of ten of those who have dominated literary sensibility in our time—weren't they not only politically silly, but politically wicked?

[3]

Didn't the influence of all they represented bring Auschwitz that much nearer?"

Snow could not

defend the indefensible . . . The honest answer was that there is, in fact, a connection which literary persons were culpably slow to see, between some kinds of early twentieth-century art and the most imbecile expressions of anti-social feeling. That was one reason, among many, why some of us turned our backs on the art, and tried to hack out a new or different way for ourselves.

A scientist by training, a writer by vocation, Snow offers himself as a unique living bridge between the two cultures. But his capacities and experience extend further than this. If we are to speak of "cultures" in the plural, there is no need to be limited to two. Administrators in the universities, in business, and government belong neither to science nor the arts, and may be considered to constitute a culture of their own. "One of the most bizarre features of any industrial society in our time," Snow wrote in *Science and Government*, "is that the cardinal choices have to be made by a handful of men . . . who cannot have a first-hand knowledge of what these choices depend upon or what their results may be." Nonscientific administrators now decide how science is to be organized and used.

During the thirties, as fellow and tutor at King's College, Cambridge, Snow saw university administration at first hand. From 1939 on, he really walked the corridors of power. He recruited scientists for the war effort and helped to decide how they were to be distributed among the competing, understaffed war agencies. After the war he was a director of the English Electric Company. When the Labor Party came to power in October, 1964, with Harold Wilson as Prime Minister, Snow was appointed Parliamentary Secretary, the second-ranking post, in the new Ministry of Technology, and was made a peer, Lord Snow of Leicester, so that he could represent the ministry in the House of Lords. All through his rapid climb, Snow never forgot that he grew up in a poor family and that his first serious education was of his own winning in a provincial, red brick, technical evening school. His background and sense of class differences bring him into natural sympathy with younger social-minded postwar writers like Amis and Osborne.

Not since Disraeli has a popular, political-minded novelist been so intimately involved with the actual exercise of power. Not since H. G. Wells has a popular, social-minded novelist known so much at first hand about science. For nearly twenty years before 1958, Snow had been in an ideal position to carry out in his fiction the program defined in "The Two Cultures." By bringing together two kinds of imagination which he had himself experienced, he could enable scientists and literary men to appreciate each other, and the lay public to appreciate both. He could dramatize for his readers the struggle toward those social goods which he condemned the major writers of his century for betraying.

But if we—by act of will—forget temporarily about "The Two Cultures" and read carefully through Snow's fiction to see what actually occurs there, we find it almost totally inconsistent with what we had been led to expect.

In all of C. P. Snow's novels taken together there is less concrete evidence of how the scientific mind works and how its methods and discoveries differ from those of the literary man or philosopher or theologian than we could find in almost any article in any issue of *Nature* or *Scientific American*. There is simply no comparison, in this respect, between his work and that of Aldous Huxley or of H. G. Wells himself.

This is not because of any intrinsic difficulties that make the new science incommunicable. While Snow's later novels were being written, the educated public was already fascinated by living cells and the role of the giant molecules in life processes. The attempts to "break" the genetic codes carried by DNA had obvious appeal to the Wellsian type of imagination. But such matters are not touched upon in any of Snow's serious fiction, even though Arthur Miles in *The Search* had seen the coming importance of the protein molecules and had decided to devote his future work to determining their structure. Except for one early, anonymous, and now unobtainable effort, Snow is emphatically not a writer of science fiction.

There are similar discrepancies in his treatment of politics. Snow's reference in "The Two Cultures" to "nine out of ten" of the writers as wickedly reactionary is extremely misleading. In the thirties, writers were very active internationally in the fight against war and Fascism. The statement by Snow—or the scientist he quotes—makes sense only if "literary sensibility" is given a very restricted and poetic meaning. Most major novelists and playwrights—and at least the younger poets—were fully engaged politically, on what Snow and his alter ego Lewis Eliot would surely regard as the right side. If we think of Mann, Silone, Barbusse, Bernanos, Aragon, Hemingway, Steinbeck, O'Casey, Spender, Dreiser, Dos Passos, Sartre, and Camus, we realize that the literary "culture" was quite as responsible and progressive politically as the scientific. In fact, in the West generally, writers were far more energetic and conspicuous than scientists in supporting the Spanish loyalists and working for a united front against Fascism.

"Strangers and Brothers" is a long series of interrelated novels all told in the first person by Lewis Eliot. In his personal friendships and partisanships, Snow's narrator is curiously indifferent to politics. "The Two Cultures" posited a connection between advanced literary sensibility and wicked political attitudes. Snow never possessed such sensibility and so could not repudiate it. But in his novels there is a remarkable tolerance for those whose "views brought Auschwitz that much closer." The man whom Lewis Eliot loves, Roy Calvert, is, during the years in which they are closest, an active pro-Nazi who tries to convert Lewis. In *The Masters* the candidate whom Lewis works to elect, a man named Jago, is ultimately defeated because of his reactionary political views. His opponents decide that they cannot afford to have such a man at the head of a college when everything for which a college should stand is being threatened by the spread of Hitlerism. Though Lewis Eliot describes himself as a left-liberal, Jago's views do not seem to disturb him in the slightest, and he supports Jago stanchly to the end. Other supporters are Roy Calvert and a Tory named Arthur Brown.

There is no reason, of course, why a character should not take a different political position from his creator, even when he is the sole reporter of all that occurs. But Lewis Eliot's relation to Snow is puzzling. Year by year, event by event, their careers are parallel, and in his general reflections on life Eliot seems to be speaking for his creator.

But why is he named Lewis Eliot? Snow, as we shall see, takes names seriously and plays on them freely. His spokesman's name links those of two of the villains mentioned most conspicuously in "The Two Cultures": Wyndham Lewis and T. S. Eliot. And yet the narrative method, which lets Lewis Eliot do all the talking and describing, without subjecting him to the kind of test that would permit us to judge his self-judgments, makes it difficult to see exactly how he is more or less than Snow's spokesman or other self. Though less bouncy and ideological and restlessly introspective, Snow's autobiographic narrative mode in *The Search* and the Lewis Eliot series is essentially that of H. G. Wells in novels like *The New Machiavelli* and *Tono Bungay*.

When H. G. Wells sent Henry James a copy of *The New*

Machiavelli, James replied with high praise, but lamented "the bad service you have done your cause by riding so hard again that accurst autobiographical form." The novelist, James said, cannot present an authentic vision unless a particular detachment operates, a detachment "terribly wanting in autobiography brought, as the horrible phrase is, up to date."

Since this detachment is wanting in the artistic form of Snow's novels, the reader must create it for himself, from the implications of what is reported and what is valued. Despite the number of novels, this is not as difficult as it might appear.

The action consists largely of talk among small groups of people. This talk is directed toward practical or emotional ends; rarely are literary, scientific, or political ideas developed for their own sake. In Snow's novels people seldom write letters, and they telephone chiefly to arrange face-to-face meetings. At these meetings something unexpected is usually revealed—often reluctantly, hesitantly, as a result of close questioning—which makes it necessary to plan at once a meeting with somebody else. If Lewis is not present, the participants arrange to see him immediately, tell him what occurred, and get his advice. Even if it is two o'clock in the morning, it is better to see Lewis Eliot then than wait until next day. We always have a meeting to look forward to, at the same time that we are absorbing the implications of one that has just occurred. The novels consist of a series of short dramatic chapters, each marking a stage in the careful step-by-step development of some issue or affair.

In recent years perhaps the most influential academic critic in England has been F. R. Leavis. In 1962 Leavis devoted his farewell lecture at Cambridge, where he had taught for many decades, to a savage personal attack on Snow. This caused even more furor than Snow's "The Two Cultures" lecture. In one of his cruder gibes, Leavis reported a rumor that Snow's novels were written by an electronic computer named Charlie to which Snow simply fed chapter titles. An enthusiast for D. H. Lawrence, Leavis said that Snow has no talent as a novelist whatsoever, and no sense of what a novel can or should be.

This is unfair. Stylistically, imaginatively, and mimetically, Snow's resources as a novelist are limited, but he husbands them carefully and employs them with conscious skill. Some of Snow's repetitions, it is true, lend themselves to parody, but by his sneer Leavis can legitimately call attention chiefly to the very traditional mode in which Snow writes. Some years ago, criticizing Henry James, Leavis found James's main weakness as novelist the result of an upbringing which kept him, for all his interest in civilization, from developing "any sense of society as a system of functions and responsibilities." This is what Snow's fiction is about.

The novelist whom Snow most resembles is Anthony Trollope. Trollope's Barsetshire novels—that series of six, beginning with *The Warden* in 1857—has many of the same ingredients as the "Strangers and Brothers" series, dramatized in the same way. Complex institutions—governmental and clerical—are staffed by the worldly, the selfish, the conscientious, the refractory, battling for principles, place, and power. Strong-minded ladies intervene in matters that should not be their concern. Official bodies examine cases whose moral complexities are almost impossible to untangle. Trollope's social range is wide, from noble lords, often of dubious morality, to ambitious young clerics from poor families. There are, as in Snow, dramatic confrontations in a series of chapters with such titles as "Mrs. Proudie Wrestles and Gets a Fall" and "The Bishops Sit Down to Breakfast." Snow's chapter titles are deliberately prosy and unenterprising. His first serious novel, *The Search*, includes "The Institute Is Talked About" and "They Discuss a Change." His most recent, *Corridors of Power*, includes "Something in the Open," "A Weekend in the Country," and "Humiliation among Friends."

In Snow's "Strangers and Brothers" series, as in Trollope's "Barsetshire" series, the same characters figure in novel after novel, now playing major roles, now minor ones. But the separate novels are self-sufficient and were not published in a sequence corresponding to the chronological sequence of the events they describe. We are free to group the novels according to their principal themes and subject matter.

It is natural to start with *The Search* (1934). This is a kind of trial autobiographical run, using a hero slightly different from Lewis Eliot (at least his name is different) but obviously drawing on the same fund of experience as the "Strangers and Brothers" series. In *Time of Hope* (1949) and *Homecoming* (1956) Lewis Eliot tells his own story up through the point at which his second marriage has been tested and proved sound. In *Strangers and Brothers* (1940), *The Light and the Dark* (1947), *The New Men* (1954), and *The Conscience of the Rich* (1958) Lewis Eliot describes the flawed lives of the four men to whom he felt closest: George Passant, Roy Calvert, his brother Martin, and Charles March. *The Masters* (1951) and *The Affair* (1960), the two most concentrated of the novels, describe how the fellows of a college at Cambridge handle two controversial cases separated by sixteen years. These novels resemble the others in the series, however, because of the temperamental inadequacies of the principals in the two cases. Finally, there is Snow's most recent novel, *Corridors of Power* (1964), product of the period of his greatest fame and public authority, with Lewis Eliot nearly as eminent as his creator.

A slightly revised edition of *The Search* was published in 1958, the year of "The Two Cultures" lecture. Snow says that he was encouraged to reissue the work because so many scientists remembered it as showing what science looked like from inside. I. I. Rabi, Nobel Prize physicist, calls it "the one novel which I knew which was really about scientists living as scientists." The introduction ends with a plea for the kind of education that will bring science and other aspects of culture into creative union.

As so often happens with works of imaginative truth, *The Search* as a novel seems to be saying something quite different and much less "constructive." The hero not only fails at science and decides that he has no true vocation for it, but in a silent act of complicity decides not to expose a friend who has violated the most basic scientific ethics.

We first see the narrator, Arthur Miles, as an eleven-year-old boy with an ineffectual, vaguely speculative father. They try to put together a telescope. When the father fumbles the placing of the lens, Arthur pretends, to save his father's feelings, that he can see more than he really does. The "personal thing," he realizes years later, counts more with him than honesty. Nevertheless, he determines to know, to learn, instead of merely wondering, like his father. Despite all sorts of discouragement Arthur wins science scholarships, and makes his way through King's College.

After taking a first in the examinations, young Miles plans his career with considerable shrewdness. Beginning in a known area in crystallography, where results are fairly certain, he will then move slowly into an unexplored area, that of the structure of the protein, where great things can be accomplished. Before his limitations, expecially in mathematics, become evident, Arthur hopes to make enough of a mark so that he can organize and direct research carried out by others.

"I shan't mind giving up working with my own hands," he tells Audrey, the girl who loves him.

"It's a waste of time when I can get people to do it better. But—I want to run the work. That's the important thing."

[11]

She frowned: "You'll like the power?"

"I think I shall," I said. I burst out: "Of course I shall, but it's not all."

After long frustrating research at Cambridge, Arthur sees a very pretty pattern emerging. In a final check of his X rays, he notices in the next-to-last one some black dots that ruin the whole scheme. He thinks, "If I had not taken this photograph, what would have happened?" He would have published his results and gone ahead. If a later researcher discovered something wrong it would have been attributed to honest error. "I suppose, for a moment, I wanted to destroy the photograph." A counterimpulse rules this out, but Arthur now understands the psychology of fraud. Frauds occur very frequently in Snow's novels. "After that afternoon, I could not help being tolerant toward them."

Later, with dramatic cabled help from a friend in Germany, he makes a genuine though modest discovery, and has a glimpse, at least, of the almost mystic joy of revelation. A friend of his, a moody young genius named Constantine, brings Arthur in as a nonvoting member of a committee planning a National Institute for Biophysical Research, with the hope that Arthur will become its director. Arthur works skillfully toward compromise among the five rather stubborn committeemen in a series of meetings less fully developed and dramatized than those in *The Masters* and *The Affair*. "I found points as I went on to meet each of their interests." But he leaves his research largely to his assistant.

Just at the crucial moment a rumor spreads that a recent paper of Arthur's will "not hold water." He spends frantic hours reviewing all the research, and comes finally upon a fact supplied by the assistant which "was wrong. Which he could not know was wrong, because there was a small technical point involved. Which I had looked over twenty times, but passed because of his assurance. Which if I had inspected it with a moment's care would have shouted itself as wrong. Upon that flaw, the whole structure rested."

Arthur loses the directorship, and has lost Audrey too. She is a restless girl, unable to settle down to anything, the line of uncertainty deepening in her forehead. Clearly she would have married Arthur if he had asked her. He returns from a period of research in Germany to find that she is going to marry his old friend Sheriff, a rather fraudulent charmer. Arthur and Audrey spend a last night of troubled physical love together, in one of Snow's most moving chapters. It is titled, interestingly enough, "Homecoming."

Arthur discovers that he has also lost his devotion to science, and wonders how genuine it had ever been. Scientific truths, though truths, are too limited. The "human" interest has become stronger.

Arthur marries a sexually inhibited woman of means, a political-minded woman, and himself writes a political invective called *The Gadarene Swine*. Preparing to leave science, and concerned about Audrey's fate, Miles tries to get Sheriff well established by giving him records of uncompleted researches. When Miles comes across Sheriff's published results in an American periodical, he sees at once that the conclusions have been faked. Arthur decides to say nothing. "And so, after the years of struggle, the personal things had won, I thought."

Scientific ethics mean less than a rather dubious personal commitment. *The Search* shows why Snow became a novelist. In his writings men are frequently judged—and judged severely—so far as specific professional qualifications for a specific responsibility are concerned. But apart from such *ad hoc* or functional judgments, his narrators seem able to accept their friends completely for what they are. Even when they hold "wicked" political views or commit fraud, the basic feeling is unaffected. This is a proper novelist's kind of sympathy, and is why Snow's novels are so readable.

The Search is an interesting novel so long as it is not regarded as an imaginative introduction to science or as a bridge between the two cultures. As a matter of fact, in most of Snow's novels, what really moves men is not the two cultures —art and science—but the need for women and the need for success. Sometimes these are in harmony, more often at war.

In The Search science comes off badly. Of the four consequential experiments, two are botched and one is faked. None is explained. We have to take on faith what lay behind the one moment of joy in discovery, and even this put in doubt by Arthur's later reflections. We have no idea what the disconcerting little dots meant in the X ray, or what "small technical point" the research assistant so disastrously overlooked.

Of The Gadarene Swine we learn even less. But it clearly stands for the two books Snow himself had written and published immediately before The Search: a detective story, Death under Sail (1932) and a science fantasy, New Lives for Old (1933), about rejuvenation and a war between Fascism and Communism.

Arthur Miles says of The Gadarene Swine: "I knew it to be fairly good, but quite a number of young men could have done it as well, and several considerably better." Neither in form or theme are Snow's own earliest publications in any way distinctive. He began by practicing the two forms of writing—the detective mystery and science fiction—most read by those who care nothing about the novel as art or truth. He learned how to handle conventional forms simply for diversion, before it occurred to him that he might use these forms to say something serious.

The murdered man in *Death under Sail* is a Harley Street cancer specialist; one of the suspects is a brilliant young doctor whose researches the specialist financed and whose ideas he appropriated, a familiar Snow motif. The young scientist-doctor is extremely able analytically and administratively, but in emotional matters a fifteen-year-old. He could "run a society, because that's really an absolutely inhuman pastime . . . but he could never run a love affair."

Though he now knew writing was his vocation, Snow did not produce his second serious novel, *Strangers and Brothers*, the first of the Lewis Eliot series, until 1940, six years after *The Search* and a year after he had thrown himself into recruiting scientists for the war effort. The first of the two autobiographical accounts of Lewis Eliot's own life, *Time of Hope*, did not appear until 1949, fifteen years after *The Search*. Though far more richly and evocatively told, Lewis Eliot's life is in outline much as Arthur Miles's.

The very first chapter is a "homecoming." After a happy picnic in a lush river setting in June, 1914, the nine-year-old Lewis is filled with panic as he returns to the incompletely understood tensions of his home. Once again the father is an ineffectual man, facing bankruptcy, quite unable to contend emotionally with his strong-minded wife and sister.

The boy's mother is romantic, superstitious, hopeful that some lucky gamble may change her fate.

On those afternoons, as we sat in the dark, the fire casting a flickering glow upon the ceiling, my mother talked to me about the hopes of her youth, her family, her snobbish ambitions, her feeling for my father, her need that I should rectify all that had gone wrong in her life.

Snow's novels return again and again—often as the only physical description—to effects of light, to fires glowing in ancient college rooms, to water shining under a night sky at a moment of lovemaking, to a single window illuminated in the darkness when someone lies gravely ill, to candles reflected in silver platters or bottles of wine or polished tables, to ornate chandeliers under which important decisions are being made.

As a result of the séances before the fire, Lewis accepts his mother's ambitions but rejects as an impossible burden the love she offers. For a long while thereafter he can only love—and is impelled to love—someone who does not love him. This unhappy need interferes with his career, keeps him from realizing the ambitions his mother inspired. Almost willfully he recreates her experience, her double frustration, on a higher level and in different form.

Inspired by George Passant's evening lectures at the local college, Lewis decides to become a lawyer. Though George arranges to have him articled to his own firm of solicitors, Lewis, on inadequate means, risks enrolling in one of the Inns of Court and preparing to be a barrister. George's anger teaches Lewis that even friends like to help on their own terms. Much later his brother Martin finds this true of Lewis also, and asks what selfishness lies beneath all Lewis's helpfulness to others.

Lewis has met Sheila Knight, a handsome, troubled girl whom none of his friends like. He falls almost instantly in love with her, as Arthur Miles had with Audrey. Sheila makes difficulties as Audrey had not. When she does finally give herself to Lewis, she says, "I don't love you, but I trust you. Get me out of this." "This" is the intolerable prison of her incapacity to love or even be at ease except with waifs and misfits. Her well-to-do parents understand Sheila even less than Lewis does. The portrait of her father, a shrewd, indirect, theatrical, hypochondriac clergyman, is one of the best of Snow's humorous, sympathetic pictures of emphatic old men.

Sheila often disappears or makes Lewis deliberately jealous. He breaks with her to concentrate on his work. Passing his examinations, he is taken as pupil into Herbert Getliffe's firm. Getliffe is a sly, muddled, successful lawyer who appropriates the researches of brilliant young assistants whom he shamelessly underpays. But with the help of his former fellow student Charles March, whose wealthy Jewish family has powerful connections, Lewis gradually establishes himself. A grinding effort of will is required, for Lewis suffers from a frightening illness of undetermined origin. He admires March and is fascinated by the world he moves in, a world more fully described in *The Conscience of the Rich*. He is determined someday to be "as sure of myself, as much able to move by instinct among the sources of information and power."

With torment over Sheila added to illness, life becomes unbearable. Lewis cannot forget her, and finally seeks her out. "I had sent her away, and now I was crawling back." It is surrender, unconditional surrender. He sees this "with absolute lucidity" and yet it is totally inconsistent with what he has always wanted of life. "I was ardent and sanguine and certain of happiness. It would have seemed incredible to hear that, in the deepest recess of my nature, I was my own prisoner." Different as Sheila is from the vulgar Mildred, this suggests the disastrous attachment in Maugham's *Of Human Bondage*.

When Lewis returns home after a difficult convalescence in France, Sheila tells him that at last she has found someone whom she can love, though she knows the man's weaknesses. We remember how Arthur Miles returned from Germany to learn that Audrey would marry the charming prevaricator Sheriff. Lewis asks Sheila what she expects of him. "See that I don't lose him."

It is a heartfelt plea, but Lewis does exactly the opposite. He puts all his lawyer's experience into scaring her lover away.

[17]

She is shattered, but finally returns to Lewis. She can no longer go it alone. Their marriage is as unhappy as what preceded it. Despite his asserted self-knowledge, Lewis is not able to act tenderly, creatively, or even acceptingly. He is full of self-pity, and appalled that his professional life is so unreal to Sheila—she cannot even pretend interest in it—and that she is so ill at ease with his friends. During the trial of George Passant for embezzlement, Lewis is so impressed by George's courage, his belief that a future is still open to him, that he decides to act as boldly. "My ambition was as imperative now as in the days when George first helped me. . . . If I died with it unfulfilled, I should die unreconciled . . . my ambition was part of my flesh and bone." He comes home from the trial to tell Sheila that he cannot bear their marriage any longer.

She takes the news stoically. This time, she tells him, there will be no return. "I have done you enough harm." But when he walks in the garden, in the moist, lime-scented air, waiting for her to finish packing, and sees the light shining from her window, he knows that he cannot let her go. "I was about to sentence myself for life." Once again "the personal things" have seemed to triumph, to prove themselves stronger than conventional ambition or the need for power. Lewis blames poor Sheila, though he had always been the pursuer. Bound to her though he is, Lewis cannot accept Sheila as he accepts the men he is fond of, and so we cannot see in her what it is he loves, sexually and otherwise. In what she says and does Sheila is often appealing and pathetic; Lewis is often contemptible. But the autobiographical method makes it difficult to know what Snow really thinks of him, or how Lewis's behavior toward Sheila is related to the almost universally admired behavior which he describes himself as exhibiting through the rest of the series.

When Lewis's autobiography is continued in *Homecoming*,

published seven years later, in 1956, we learn how brief the self-imposed life sentence turns out to be.

It is now 1938, five years after the reconciliation that ended *Time of Hope*. Lewis has modified his ambitions because of the difficulties of his marriage. Five days a week he lives comfortably as fellow and lecturer on law in a Cambridge college. Two days he spends in London with Sheila and as legal consultant to a high-powered manufacturer named Lufkin.

It is hard on Sheila, who tries desperately to fill her loneliness. Lewis's homecomings are attended with the same kind of anxiety he recalled from childhood at the beginning of *Time of Hope*. He is encouraged when Sheila uses her independent income to back a courtly, unscrupulous, once-distinguished literary man in a publishing venture. She is even able to put some of her secret thoughts on paper with a book in mind. But the publisher, one of the more complex and interesting of the many self-defeating characters in Snow's novels, hates to seek patronage and circulates malicious stories about Sheila and Lewis. When Lewis confronts him, he seems relieved and promptly returns Sheila's money. But for Shelia the exposure is too great, the wound too deep. A few months later, while Lewis is off having dinner with a friend, she commits suicide.

Charles March, now a doctor, tries to be helpful, but there are terrible scenes with Sheila's parents. Lewis, himself, feels an unbearable need to speak to Sheila which, in his total lack of religious faith, he knows never can be satisfied. A quarter of the way through, the novel seems to come to an end.

Two years later, in 1939, when Lewis is working in a war ministry, he meets Margaret Davidson, daughter of a prominent art critic, and falls almost at once into a spontaneous, apparently happy love affair. She discovers, however, that

Lewis had not told her of Sheila's suicide, and wonders how free emotionally he really is.

"With anyone who wants you altogether" [Margaret tells him] "you are cruel. Because one never knows when you're going to be secretive, when you're going to withdraw. With most people you're good, but in the end you'll break the heart of anyone who loves you."

They begin drifting apart. Suddenly, without warning, she reveals that she is going to marry a capable young doctor. She does so and has a child. For over two years, Lewis knows nothing of her life. But once he has worked out in his mind what was wrong in his attitude toward Margaret, he sets out to win her back, deliberately, patiently, step by step. At a clandestine meeting at a restaurant, Margaret sits smiling in the aura of a table lamp, "her face open and softened, as though breathing in the present moment. When I first met her, I had been enraptured by her capacity for immediate joy, and so I was now." We remember that once Sheila pressed Lewis to tell her what, if anything, he really believed in and what he would sacrifice for his beliefs. They had been talking of one of George Passant's employers who gave up all his possessions to become an itinerant preacher. Defensively Lewis tossed the question back to Sheila. She said, curiously enough, that she believed "in joy."

Lewis arranges Margaret's divorce, though people close to both Lewis and Margaret think he is wrong to do so. He persists, they are married, have a child, and seem happy. He must, however, pay a price. Their child falls ill with an infection of the brain. When Charles March makes a wrong diagnosis, for apparently excusable technical reasons, Margaret's first husband, with more recent advanced training, is called in, and the child is saved, with much spiritual purgation for all concerned. Despite his interest in science, Snow fails to explain exactly what the clinical situation is, or the reasons for Charles's mistake.

On the way back from the hospital Lewis notices a scent of lime blossom beneath the smell of hot grass and traffic fumes.

We were in sight of home. A light was shining in one room: the others stood black, eyeless, in the leaden light. It was a home-coming such as, for years, I thought I was not to know. Often in my childhood, I had felt dread as I came near home. It had been worse when I went, as a young man, toward the Chelsea house. Now, walking with Margaret, that dread had gone.

They live happily ever after. In later novels, Margaret is entirely the admiring, reassuring, understanding companion. There is never a hint of any serious conflict between them or in their feelings about each other. The nature of their sexual life is left discreetly unrecorded.

In the four novels devoted to each of the four men closest to him, Lewis mentions his own concerns only obliquely, presenting himself entirely as friend or brother. "Not by virtue but simply by temperament, I was bound by chains to anyone who had ever really touched my life; once they had taken hold of me, they had taken hold for good." In each novel Lewis gives himself up single-mindedly, in a Jamesian way, to playing the role of observer, intermediary, and confidant in another man's life. Because of this, we tend to forget, when Lewis is concentrating on George Passant, say, or Roy Calvert, how deeply involved he may be at the same time with Martin Eliot or Charles March or with Sheila or Margaret. In the interests of dramatic simplicity, Snow sacrifices the complex interweaving of themes and relations that the general design of his series —inspired, he suggests, by Proust—ought to encourage.

Strangers and Brothers, the first and weakest of these four portraits, is about George Passant. Lewis always thinks of

[21]

George as built along the lines of a great man, but no evidence supports this. The novel begins with a chapter characteristically titled "Firelight on a Silver Cigarette Case." The case, esoterically designed, has been given to Jack Cotery, a member of George's group (or coterie) by fifteen-year-old Roy Calvert, who has a crush on him. Roy's father, Jack's employer, is ready to ease Jack out of his job and cut off his firm-sponsored scholarship. Though it may get him into trouble professionally in the town, George fights the matter vigorously in a school committee, with Lewis Eliot—of course—serving temporarily as secretary. As usual in Snow's novels, a not fully satisfactory compromise results.

In the course of the next five years, George becomes involved with Jack in various side activities. They take over an advertising weekly, acquired earlier by the former member of George's law firm who has become a religious fanatic. They buy the farm where George and his disciples meet weekends, and turn it into a hostel, intended to be the first of a chain. After borrowing money privately—from women mostly—for these enterprises, they run into real trouble when some of those from whom they borrowed prosecute them for misrepresentation.

Since this is a small city, a serious scandal is in the making. Sexual relations within the group have become complicated. George, who is a man of strong passions, had always sought release by picking up girls on the street in Nottingham, or going to low dives there. More and more, after the group acquires the farm, he makes love fairly promiscuously with girls whom he takes there for weekends.

The trial raises questions of honest understanding of one's own motives similar to those confronting Arthur Miles in *The Search*. George tends to push from his mind uncomfortable facts, as Arthur Miles was tempted to do when his beautiful research results were threatened. Jack Cotery blithely makes use of falsehood, as Sheriff had done.

At the trial, Herbert Getliffe saves Jack and George from an unfavorable verdict, but not from scandal. At the last moment the religious wanderer turns up to confess that it was he who gave a wrong impression of the weekly paper's circulation figures because he was so eager to be free of it. Sympathizing with the jury's condemnation of the sexual life at the farm, Getliffe still manages to make it seem symptomatic of the war-caused disorientation of the twenties.

George Passant is furious at this defense. It denies his dignity as a man, his existential freedom. After a generous sampling of his vapid diary entries the reader can hardly take George Passant as seriously as Lewis and the author seem to. This is the tumultuous late twenties and early thirties, but George's allegedly powerful analytic mind is unengaged by the books, ideologies, and political events abroad which preoccupied practically all the ardent young of that period. Nor is he tested in the hurly-burly of left-wing politics.

Though he had marked time professionally in the nine years before the trial, George finds his justification in the existence of the group. The final, painful, unanswered question of the novel is whether he has not been deceiving himself about the motives and character of his influence. Is his persisting courage and self-confidence after the trial possible only because his self-accounting is flawed? Once again the narrative method makes it hard to judge. Does Snow admire the mind behind these diaries as much as Lewis Eliot seems to, or is he giving us the portrait of a sentimental, self-protective fornicator moving into middle age?

Lewis Eliot's profoundest friendship is with Roy Calvert. In 1933, after he begins living most of the week at the Cambridge college where Roy, now twenty-four, is a research student in Middle Eastern languages, they see each other once or twice a day on terms of warm intimacy. Roy's tenderness, raillery, and grace charm nearly everyone, but especially women. He is close to Lady Muriel, wife of the gravely ill master of the college; to Joan, her daughter; and to their amusing, snobbish relatives Lord and Lady Bocastle. Lewis is drawn into these circles too, where the conversation is worldly, witty, and sharp-edged, as it had not been in the series before.

Roy is nearly as desperate within himself as Sheila, but he is far more articulate in explaining his problem and more varied and theatrical in seeking relief from it. He has an absolute conviction of isolation from God. "It's much more real than anything one can see or touch—that God and His world exist. And everyone can enter and find their rest. Except me. I'm infinitely far away for ever."

Roy's deep spiritual malaise finds expression in provocative academic behavior; in trips to Germany because of fascination with Nazism; and in a series of affairs sufficiently numerous and conspicuous to affect his chance of a fellowship. When, for instance, an old scholar who does not deserve it is being honored at a grand testimonial meeting, Roy devastatingly and with pretended innocence speaks of the scholar's long-dead young collaborator from whose unpublished literary remains and without acknowledgment the scholar almost certainly wrote his one substantial book.

Roy goes frequently to Germany, lives there in a nether world like that described in Isherwood's *Mr. Norris Changes Trains*. Roy and Lewis's disagreement about Nazism has no effect on their friendship, even though Roy tries deliberately to convert Lewis. Roy's sense of the inadequacies of the communist and left-liberal view of life is precisely what caused the politically "wicked" views of the modern writers whom Snow

[24]

attacks in "The Two Cultures." Lewis Eliot—and Snow—can sympathize with this in Roy, and yet not understand its far profounder expression in Yeats, in Pound, in Eliot, in Lawrence.

Eliot's reason for loving Roy is more convincing than his love for Margaret or Sheila. We have more detailed awareness of Roy's physical presence in a room, his manner, his appearance. The conversational exchanges are richer. Of a walk near the college Lewis says fervently:

We talked on, so attuned that each word resounded in the other's heart. And at the same moment that I felt closer to him than I had ever done, I was seized and shaken by the most passionate sense of his nature, his life, his fate. It was a sense which shook me with resentment, fear and pity, with horror and unassuageable anxiety, with wonder, illumination and love. I accepted his nature with absolute gratitude . . . to know him was one of the two greatest gifts in my life.

He is quite frank about the quality of this feeling. He says of Roy that "with his first-hand knowledge of life, he knew that any profound friendship must contain a little of the magic of love. And he was always as physically spontaneous as an Italian."

Through most of the novel Roy is involved in a triangular relationship with Joan and with a hardheaded, pretty, socially insecure girl named Rosalind. Young, untried, awkward, passionate, Joan gives herself totally in love for Roy until he breaks abruptly with her. In the chapter about Joan called "A Young Woman in Love," the heightened prose suggests abandonment of the usual narrative indirection in favor of something close to omniscience. During Roy and Joan's love affair, Rosalind rather surprisingly becomes engaged to a clergyman protégé of Roy's. After the outbreak of the war, even more surprisingly, Roy marries her. They have a child, and it makes him happy enough to regret the suicidal wish that led him to

[25]

pull wires to get into a bomber brigade.

Before Roy's inevitable death in combat, he and Lewis go on a strange melodramatic trip to Spain and across occupied France to Switzerland to make contact with former German friends of Roy's who might possibly be putting out significant peace feelers. The mission comes to nothing, but Eliot and Roy have one more intense period together.

The Light and the Dark lacks a political theme, has little to say about morality or society. Lewis discusses Nazism very abstractly, with no analysis of specific European developments or personalities, though he takes his usual interest in practical academic politics. It is a question of whether Roy, specialist in the recently recovered language Soghdian, should be elected a fellow, in preference to a productive young proletarian scientist named Walter Luke. But the novel is primarily a love story, as the concluding poignant memory of Roy directly tells us.

The New Men (1954) is a story of brothers, of Lewis and Martin Eliot. The sudden importance of Martin—nine years younger than Lewis—is a little startling. He has barely been mentioned in the series since their mother was indignantly pregnant with him a quarter of a century earlier in *Time of Hope*. Preoccupied with careers, Lewis Eliot and Arthur Miles ignored their families. We have no sense of how Martin grew up or what role, if any, he played during the difficult years with Sheila.

Nor is it clear why at this point Snow introduces his scientist brother as the "new man" when the series already contains first-rate scientists like Walter Luke and Francis Getliffe, Herbert Getliffe's younger brother. Is it an opportunity to split Snow's self-image in the novels into two halves to dramatize the quarrel within the self?

But the split, so interpreted, becomes very confusing. Lewis accuses Martin of cold, ruthless, calculating ambition, though Martin strikes the reader as impetuous and variable, shifting from one extreme position to its opposite. Martin accuses Lewis of being too self-indulgent in personal relations, of wasting himself in them, just at the time when Lewis is moving most rapidly and forcefully into a position of influence.

These are the war years. A cousin of Lord Bocastle, put in charge of coordinating confidential scientific work, chooses Lewis Eliot as his personal assistant. A series of crises and decisions follows, presented without much thematic coherence. Should research into nuclear fission be pushed, and specifically the research directed by Martin Eliot and Walter Luke, even after the heartbreaking failure of their first atomic pile? Later Luke and a young scientist named Sawbridge nearly die of radiation sickness. When America throws its tremendous resources into making the bomb, should Britain close up Harwell (or Barford, as it is called here) and use its scientists in other much needed ways? Finally America explodes the bomb, and then drops it on Hiroshima and Nagasaki. Almost to a man, according to Lewis Eliot, British scientists find the bombings unnecessary and indefensible. They feel betrayed. Should they protest, and how?

On his own, Martin composes a strong letter to the *Times* which would certainly finish him for any public office. Lewis dissuades him from sending it. But when Sawbridge is suspected of leaking information to the Russians, Martin puts all his energies into breaking him down. Lewis angrily accuses Martin of playing this role to curry official favor and be made next head of Barford instead of Walter Luke, who scorns what he considers American-style fanaticism about security and Soviet spies.

When the post is offered him, Martin Eliot at the last moment turns it down. He wants to be free to think and speak as a man, not an official. The decision also shows that he is free of his youthful need to rival his older brother. And now his relationship with his wife is secure too. Against Lewis's advice, Martin had married Irene, an attractive, restless, vulnerable girl, much like Audrey or Sheila. Through most of the novel she is still involved with a lover out of her past, a slightly disreputable journalist who recalls Sheriff and some of the men to whom Sheila was attracted. Irene is able to give herself fully to Martin when she realizes that he loves her out of strength, not weakness. This provides the confidence that her deep self-distrust had never before let her feel, or even believe possible.

Though he sacrifices a top post in administration, to return to teaching science in competition with younger men more brilliant than he, Martin seems happy. But the novel fails in its attempt to present Martin's emotions, his science, and his dramatic shifts of position through his brother's eyes. Martin is too reticent with Lewis for that. The science is inadequately explained, and the presumably dramatic inner life is seen only at one or two removes. Martin does not capture Lewis's imagination—or ours—as Roy Calvert does, or Sheila Knight.

The Conscience of the Rich (1958) also dramatizes renunciation and a quarrel between kin, in this case the painful widening breach between Charles March and his father. The Marches are an old, far-flung and respected Jewish banking family whose members in rotation entertain each other at huge dinners on Friday nights. Into this fascinating world Lewis Eliot is warmly received, and soon plays his usual confidant's role, especially with Charles's elderly widowed father, a talkative worrier with total recall. Mr. March is a mad, impetuous character who ranks as a creation with Sheila Knight's father.

Though he has a keener legal mind than Lewis Eliot's, Charles gives up law as soon as he has proved his ability at it. He cannot face the kind of success that his family connections will place in his lap. But a decision to become a doctor, after two years of restless, fashionable idleness, troubles his father even more. Mr. March decides to cut off Charles's inheritance. He rightly interprets his son's decision as a criticism of his own mode of life. "He could not begin to understand the sense of social guilt, the sick conscience, which were real in Charles." He suspects correctly that Charles has been influenced by Ann Simon, daughter of a wealthy Jewish physician. Ann is a Communist and supporter of a weekly, *Note*, edited by Humphrey Seymour, a witty upper-class ideologue. *Note* is modeled on *The Week*, edited by Claud Cockburn.

Mr. March had a series of shocks when Charles gave up law, when his daughter Katherine married a Gentile, Francis Getliffe, and when Charles married Ann Simon. Worse is in store. *Note* is using scandal, some of it rather dubious, to try to bring down the present government of appeasers. Part of this scandal concerns Herbert Getliffe and Mr. March's brother, Sir Philip, who holds a government post. Ann is in a position to stop what *Note* is doing, but Charles will not try to influence her. Both she and Seymour are, according to Lewis Eliot, "believers by nature. At times it gave them a purity and innocence that men like Charles never knew: at times it gave Seymour, and perhaps even Ann, a capacity to do things from which Charles, answering to his own conscience, would have been repelled."

When Ann falls dangerously ill, she rather implausibly provides Lewis Eliot with information for Charles to have after her death; it will enable him to stop *Note* if he wishes. After she begins to recover, she sends Charles, even more implausibly, to learn from Lewis what the information was. "She'd rather you told me than tell me herself."

At a big family conference Charles refuses to use the weapon in his hands. Though he is not a Communist and loves his father and sister, his respect for the integrity of Ann's beliefs is so great that he will not stop what *Note* is doing. The attitude is essentially unpolitical, as was Lewis Eliot's emotional acceptance of Roy Calvert at the time that Roy was a Nazi.

When he lets "personal things" be dominant for Charles, when he lets him be governed chiefly by respect for Ann's faith, Snow both avoids and confuses the issues. To stop *Note*, Charles would have had to turn over to the authorities certain documents in Ann's possession which *Note* had obtained improperly. This could have raised the whole troubling question—a central one for Koestler, Orwell, and Sartre—of liberal support of Communists, especially where the uglier aspects of Communist totalitarianism are concerned. Because Charles keeps silent for love of Ann, the issue is left in the same moral obscurity as the issue of Arthur Miles's integrity when he failed to reveal Sheriff's fraud.

The Conscience of the Rich is not a political novel; it is a study of Charles March's character. As in *The New Men*, the narrative method is an obstacle to understanding. Lewis tells us that Charles, like himself, had trouble accepting and reciprocating love, but the only woman we see him with is Ann, and they are in apparently complete rapport. We are told that Charles "had always been fascinated by the idea of goodness. Was it because he was living constantly with a part of himself which he hated?" But what he hated is not dramatized. Lewis is typically present with Mr. March and Sir Philip when a dispatch box arrives from the Prime Minister containing Sir Philip's dismissal from office. But he is not present in the depths of Charles's soul, where a successful struggle goes on for goodness, and against cruelty, isolation, and pride. All that is veiled from us.

In these four novels—*Strangers and Brothers, The Dark and the Light, The New Men,* and *The Conscience of the Rich*—four men turn aside, because of deeply personal needs or problems, from the kind of success that their situations and superior talents seem to offer. Until he enters government service during the war and begins a second career, this is Lewis Eliot's history also.

The Masters (1951), the most popular of Snow's novels, is a highly concentrated, step-by-step account of a college election, but it really fits the same pattern. Lewis Eliot throws himself completely into the attempt to get Paul Jago elected because he has so much more "humanity" than the aloof, correct, unimaginative scientist who is his rival. Jago is painfully eager for the job; when his chances are threatened, his friends redouble their efforts because they think defeat will destroy Jago as a man. Later, in *Corridors of Power,* Lewis acknowledges that support for Jago was wrong. "Sometimes my affections ran away with me. . . . They had made me forget function, or justice, or even the end to be served."

The novel begins with word that the master of the college is gravely ill of inoperable cancer; it ends when a new master is sworn in. All scenes take place in the college, all bear upon the contest. The highly limited, localized contest becomes a paradigm for nonviolent power struggles within all social institutions everywhere.

Immediately on news of the master's illness, parties form. Lewis Eliot, Roy Calvert, Arthur Brown, and Brown's friend Chrystal all support Jago. Arthur Brown, the tutor, loves to maneuver in the background, effect compromises, keep the college running well. Chrystal is a strong, statesmanlike char-

[31]

acter whose name, we learn at the final vote, is Charles Percy Chrystal. (C. P. Snow is Charles Percy Snow. The first sentence of the novel begins, "The snow had only just stopped . . ." Snow is made of crystals. It is in crystallography that Arthur Miles, Snow's first alter ego, begins his research.)

With Lewis Eliot presenting the situation, our interest focuses almost entirely on the lively play of personalities, not on substantive issues. Curriculum, educational theories, university government, student problems are hardly mentioned. Francis Getliffe does rebuke Lewis for supporting, in 1937, a stubborn conservative instead of the liberal Crawford, but the issue is then dropped until near the end. The student protest movements and the heated intricate political arguments that would have been going on in that year are totally ignored.

Tension is increased because the master lives longer than was expected and because he must be shielded from knowledge of the electioneering. All antagonisms, hopes, and self-questionings are exacerbated. Should promotions to other posts be used for bargaining? How much pressure should be put on young Luke, who does not have tenure? Should Jago be told to persuade his wife to stop acting as if she were already mistress of the master's lodge?

Every casual meeting is a contest. Private conversations, especially between those in opposite factions, arouse curiosity and suspicion. By the time the election takes place a great many ample dinners have been eaten in which the fellows have succeeded or failed in maintaining gentlemanly relations between the factions; much fine wine has been contributed ceremoniously by individual fellows to honor this occasion or that. At times the obsession with the coming election seems slightly mad; the fellows appear to do nothing but caucus and eat.

An unsuccessful scientist named Nightingale, still expecting his totally unlikely election to the Royal Society, shifts his support from Jago to Crawford and begins circulating malicious statements about Jago's wife. Nightingale's early defection is followed much later by the return from Europe of Pilbrow, an elderly lighthearted *bon vivant*, who has been abroad during most of the maneuvering. Alarmed by the success of Nazism, he is absolutely opposed to putting in office someone with Jago's political views. At the last moment, for quite different reasons, Chrystal decides that he must support Crawford, though this means a painful rupture with his old friend Brown.

Jago takes defeat very hard, but when he forces himself to drink the health of the new master there is a sense of restored unity, of corporate survival. Other novels of the series have concentrated on individuals governed by impulses they could neither control nor fully understand. Now a group of such individuals, still so governed, decide on the future of the college. In such a committee process do the irrational personal motives cancel each other out? Do sensible men, acting democratically, usually reach sensible decisions?

This question is debated again, somewhat repetitiously, in *The Affair*, (1960) set in the same college sixteen years later, with an overlapping cast of characters. Again an election for master is in prospect, with Arthur Brown and Francis Getliffe as the likely choices. But the fellows are more immediately split over a case that is as unrepresentative and as curious in its details as the charges against George Passant for swindling.

A rude, resentful, provisional fellow, Howard, of leftist leanings, has been quietly dropped for falsifying the scientific data in his thesis. He and his wife, a handsome Communist who sees human beings totally in strategic and ideological terms, campaign for a reconsideration of the case. Naturally they try to involve Lewis Eliot, an important man of affairs, but still close to the college, where Martin is now a fellow.

[33]

The issue is complicated not only by the prospective election of master but by the fact that nearly everyone dislikes Howard. Some of the conservatives feel justified in considering his political views, since they believe a Communist to be incapable of honesty. They charge, unfairly, that the liberals and leftists support Howard for political reasons. Since the war the proportion of conservatives has greatly increased.

The facts are hard to get at. Howard had done his research under an old scientist, now dead, uncle-in-law of one of the fellows. A photograph on which Howard's conclusions were based is discovered to have been "blown up" so that the dimensions are erroneous. An American notices that the tack hole, caused when the original negative was hung up to dry, is too large! This is about all the "science" we are vouchsafed. As usual, the character of the experiment on which so much depends is not explained.

By a circuitous route the old scientist's papers reach the college authorities. At some point a photograph has been removed from one of the notebooks. The inscription under it suggests that it might be the crucial photograph which Howard says he reproduced exactly as his professor gave it to him. Howard proves to be an exasperating witness in the hearings at which Lewis Eliot serves as his legal adviser. He is vague, truculent, can never give a straight answer. And he must be a poor scientist to hang everything on unchecked data supplied by somebody else. Finally Francis Getliffe, with his great authority, decides that it was not Howard who faked the photograph, and the case ends in a rather unsatisfactory compromise.

The facts are messy, unpleasing to all, including the reader. By calling the novel, a little pretentiously, The Affair, Snow recalls the Dreyfus case, but in that case the ideological and social alignments—clerical and anticlerical, liberal and reactionary, socialist and traditionalist—were very clear. The baffling facts and Howard's unsatisfactory explanations suggest rather Trollope's *The Last Chronicle of Barset*, where Mr. Crawley has to surrender his incumbency when he gives so unsatisfactory an explanation of how he came by a lost or stolen twenty-pound check which he deposited to his account. He, also, is later exonerated.

The lack of clarity in the Howard case permits us once again to concentrate on the personal issues and the process itself.

As before, Nightingale is the villain. Handling him so as to achieve justice and yet not create an open scandal is a delicate business for Lewis and the Court of Seniors. Readers of *The Masters* are naturally interested to see how old acquaintances have fared. Under Crawford's mastership Arthur Brown has retained his quiet power. Chrystal is dead. Jago makes a brief, effective foray from the bitterness of his retirement. Gay, the aged, ebullient, Norse saga man of *The Masters* is incredibly still alive, still demanding to be heard.

The Affair too greatly resembles *The Masters*, and suffers the disadvantages of a sequel or reprise. Howard is poor stuff compared even to the overeager, insecure Jago.

In *Corridors of Power* (1964), on the other hand, Snow treats a public issue more directly and clearly than in *The New Men*, describing the exercise of great power on nearly the highest governmental level. Once again the "personal thing" gets in the way.

This time the central figure is not an old friend or brother, though plenty of old friends are involved, most of them now as titled and prominent as their creator, Lord Snow. Walter Luke and Francis Getliffe are knights; Lewis Eliot's former employer, Lufkin, who has steadily increased his industrial empire since the war, is a Lord, and Horace Timberlake, whose possible benefaction to the college was a complicating factor in *The Masters*, is Viscount Bridgewater. Now, in 1955, Lewis Eliot has been working for sixteen years as a fictionally convenient kind of free-lance assistant to Sir Hector Rose, Permanent Secretary of one of the war ministries. Rose, like most of the younger civil servants, is solidly conservative. A Tory government holds office.

The central character is Roger Quaife whom we first see pressing Lewis's good American friend, the physicist David Rubin, on the matter of nuclear policy. The name Rubin suggests that of Snow's friend I. I. Rabi. Quaife is particularly concerned with the arms race between the United States and Russia, and what kind of significant role, if any, Britain can play in preventing disasters.

A faithful reader of the whole Lewis Eliot series is not surprised that one of the first things Roger Quaife does, as soon as he is given a junior ministerial post, is to telephone Lewis Eliot and ask whether they might, in the next few days, "spend a bachelor evening at his club." Roger talks frankly to Lewis about power and the uses of power. Before he can act significantly in the atomic arms race, he must maneuver his way into a major governmental post.

"Remember," said Roger, "there are going to be real decisions. There won't be many of them, they're only too real. People like you, sitting outside, can influence them a bit, but you can't make them. Civil servants can't make them. So far as that goes, as a junior Minister, I can't make them. To make the real decisions, one's got to have the real power."

"Are you going to get it?" I asked.

"If I don't," said Roger, "this discussion has been remarkably academic."

Lewis sets up for Roger an advisory committee of scientists,

[36]

including the villain of the book, Brodzinski, a Polish refugee scientist of ability and fanatical determination. The inclusion of Brodzinski alarms Getliffe and Luke. In Luke's view Brodzinski is "a mad Pole, whose only uncertainty was whether he hated Russians as Russians more than Russians as Communists, and who would cheerfully die himself along with the entire population of the United States and Great Britain, so long as there wasn't a Russian left alive." Quaife persuades the others that to exclude Brodzinski would be to announce prematurely in what direction he hopes to direct policy.

Again after the Suez crisis he has to give Lewis and some of the others a little lecture on political realities. Thoroughly opposed though he was to the British military seizure, thinking it wrong and futile, Roger had kept silent at the time. He knew he could do no good, and he was determined not to endanger his position with the party and thus make impossible any effective action on the atomic bomb.

After a quiet interval, the uncontrollable Brodzinski suddenly begins making speeches in America attacking his British scientist colleagues. David Rubin tells Quaife that both the United States and Russia prefer to keep atomic bomb manufacture to themselves, but that the United States would take it amiss if Britain seemed to be getting out of the atomic race for wrong or neutralist reasons, "to be sliding out of the Cold War."

In the prevailing climate of opinion it is easy for Brodzinski to arouse suspicion in America. Snow often refers in his later novels to the American anticommunist obsession. Of a rich young American courting Francis Getliffe's daughter, Lewis Eliot says, "He could not get over his discovery that Sir Francis, so eminent, so strait-laced about domestic behavior was, when he talked about the world, by American standards wildly radical . . . " Lewis thinks that it will do an American

[37]

no harm "to hear us talk about Communists as though they were human beings."

As a result of Brodzinski's charges, Quaife's advisers are double-checked by one of the security heads. Getliffe is furious, and at first refuses to go through it. Though Lewis manages to persuade him, it casts a shadow over their friendship. Lewis is angry with himself for seeming too conciliatory in his own interview. He had protested only at one circumstantial but false charge coming from an unidentified source which he assumed "was one of your ex-communists."

In the interview Lewis refers to his engagement in political activities in the thirties, to speeches at I.L.P. meetings, for instance, which had not been dramatized in the novels. Again it is evident that Snow's purposes as a novelist do not include factional politics of the sort described by Orwell and Koestler. Lewis is candid about his attitude toward Russia. He had differed with Ann March and others over the "major horrors of power."

I always believed that the power was working two ways. They were doing good things with it, as well as bad. When once they got some insight into the horrors, then they might create a wonderful society. I now believe that, more confidently than I ever did. How it will compare with the American society, I don't know. But so long as they both survive, I should have thought that many of the best human hopes stand an excellent chance.

Despite Rubin's advice, Quaife, who has now become a privy councilor, decides to press ahead. Snow suggests that it is difficult for an ambitious man to analyze his own motives at such a time. Having a real cause makes him feel better about his ambition, gives him more confidence, provides him with arguments, and if he wins, puts him in the history books. Statesmanship and self-interest are not necessarily enemies.

Meanwhile, as in all Snow's novels, the "personal thing" has intervened. Roger's wife is vivid, wealthy, intelligent, the

[38]

daughter of an earl, and effectively eager to help him win the highest position. But in mid-course he reveals confidentially to Lewis Eliot that he is in love with the former wife of a mentally ill colleague. He enlists Lewis's aid because the woman, Ellen, is being harassed by some unidentified person who knows their secret and might conceivably use it to do great harm politically. Lewis sees her alone and with Quaife a number of times. Between Roger and Ellen "there was a link of the senses, so strong that sitting with them was like being in a field of force. Why it was so strong, I should probably never know." The "probably" is amusing on a number of counts.

In a review of one of Upton Sinclair's "weirdly readable" late novels, Snow, after remarking on Lanny Budd's "preposterous intimacy with the great," says, "I suspect that all addicts of this series (me among them) secretly wish to have been Lanny Budd." Being Lewis Eliot is next best.

Snow's heart is in the right place, but his mind recoils from the highly structured or differentiated. When Snow was interviewed on television by Malcolm Muggeridge in 1962, the following exchange occurred:

Muggeridge: How Left would you regard yourself politically, Charles, in terms of our set-up here?

Snow: Well, I think the word's almost ceased to have meaning in our set-up here, hasn't it? I mean it's perfectly reasonable to be a Conservative in the present flavour of the Conservative Party (of the front bench of the Conservative Party at least), or a member of the Labour front bench, and there's almost nothing between it. For certain things I believe, as a matter of fact, that the Conservative Party could have done and in some ways have done slightly better than the Labour Party would have done for ten years.

Muggeridge: But you haven't, in the context of this country got any very strong political feeling?

Snow: No, not in the context of this country, no. In a sort of world context, certainly yes. That is, I am strongly for the poor.

[39]

Such bland generalities are apparently no disadvantage either to Snow or his alter ego. Everyone in the novels regards Lewis Eliot as both shrewd and wise, and seeks his advice. Since the reader is taken into confidence too, this is all highly informative. When, for instance, Francis Getliffe arranges a last luncheon at his club with his reckless, rebellious young daughter off on her own to America, Lewis, of course, must make a third.

Lord Lufkin, the airplane manufacturer, puts on a prestigious dinner party for political purposes. When the guests—"the Ministers, the tycoon, the Second Secretary, the P.R.S."—rise from table to go to the drawing room, Lufkin calls out sharply, "Wait a minute, Lewis, I want a word with you." Lewis leaves the party to seek Quaife, carrying a confidential message from Lufkin. Quaife, whose wife has now been informed of his affair, telephones Ellen. It is past one in the morning. He returns to say flatly to Lewis, "She wants me to go and see her. She asked me to bring you too!"

On the weekend at Bassett, a dispatch box arrives requiring immediate attention, and a secret meeting convenes in a bedroom. But the great are not comfortable without Lewis Eliot's presence. A handwritten note comes from the chief adviser to the Prime Minister: "I should be grateful if you could spare us a few minutes of your time. It would be a convenience if you could come without delay."

If these were daydreams, they anticipated what was to happen in real life. In an interview with the press in October, 1964, the new Lord Snow of Leicester—formerly C. P. Snow, later Sir Charles Snow—told how his promotion occurred.

"The Sunday after the election," Lord Snow said, "I received a phone call from 10 Downing Street, asking if I could see the Prime Minister in an hour's time. He offered me the post, and I asked for a night to think it over. Then I said yes."

The position he was offered, that of Parliamentary Secretary, was the same rank Roger Quaife held in the first part of *Corridors of Power*. Snow revealed that he did not plan to write any more novels for a while.

When *Corridors of Power* was published, Snow's political career on a ministerial level lay ahead of him. In the novel, Quaife's career comes to an end. After the long debate in Parliament, there are enough abstentions to indicate lack of confidence. Whether veiled allusions to Quaife's private life by one of the speakers had an effect is a question. Across the pool of light from a reading lamp in a darkened office, Roger reads to Lewis the draft of his letter of resignation. Clearly Roger believes deeply in what he tried to do. If he had not believed so deeply, he might have fared better. He also really loves Ellen, who is no Christine Keeler. When he divorces his wife his constituents no longer return him to Parliament. But the new marriage seems firm and good. Like Martin Eliot, he accepts with equanimity his greatly lessened position; like George Passant, he has not given up hope for himself or his ideas.

The novel ends *diminuendo*, not with politics but with personal relationships and moods: "The memory of the struggle, even the reason for it, dimmed down. We talked of the children and we were happy. . . . We talked as though the future were easy and secure, and as though their lives would bring us joy."

Despite the wistful irony, "happy" and "joy" are the proper terms. Ever since Sheila said that she believed in joy, we have known that the series was primarily concerned with individual happiness. Those characters are happy who are realistic about the chances of attaining what they seek, who can renounce ambition when it sets too high an inner price, who can suffer limitation and even defeat without bitterness. They choose

[41]

marriage and parenthood because they value them for the right reasons and are clear about what may be expected in return. A surprising number of the principals in Snow's novels achieve happiness on these moderate and even stoic terms.

Joy is another matter. Joy is not the child of measure and compromise. It is Dionysian, ecstatic, and brooks no barriers. It occurs when the self is in free, outgoing, confident rapport with ideas, objects, persons, situations, and moments. In Snow's novels it springs chiefly from science, sex, or success.

Of what particularly produces these first two kinds of joy we have only glimpses or glimmerings. We meet joyful lovers as we meet joyful scientists, but the rites of the bed are as veiled from us as the rites of the laboratory. Snow is no Puritan; neither is he D. H. Lawrence or Henry Miller. Lewis Eliot alludes fairly frankly to his early and more troubled relations with women, though with no physical details. As the series continues, gentlemanly reticence becomes total. After he marries Margaret Davidson, we should as little expect to learn specifically about their sex life or even about any serious emotional difficulties between them as to learn similar facts from the *Times* about the royal couple.

Aside from general references to sex and sickness, the physical life shared by men, plants, and animals counts for little in Snow's imagination. The sufferings of the war years are not recreated, or the excitements of combat or hunting or swimming. No one kills a bull or climbs Kilimanjaro, or plants crops or—even in laboratories—does much with his hands. To link Snow and Tolstoy, as one or two critics have done, seems particularly strange when we consider the openness, the geographic expanse of Tolstoy's world, and the wide range of emotional, sensory, intellectual, and religious experience.

A comparison with Proust, which Snow himself invites, also reveals more contrast than kinship. Proust's sensibility is richest in areas where Snow is unresponsive—in, for instance, painting, music, architecture, botany, women's dresses, philology, literary style, Bergsonian metaphysics. Proust's richly charged imaginative evocations, working through analogy and association, require a nuanced and involved prose totally unrelated to Snow's simple and sometimes careless plainspeaking. Snow has a handful of favorite figures—"lemur-eyed," for example—which he works rather hard. Even analogies drawn from science occur more in Proust than in Snow, and where Snow's version of the Dreyfus case is confined to a few college fellows, Proust shows the anti-Dreyfusard poison spreading all through the veins of French society.

A third joy is the joy of success—competitive success in examinations, in court, in bureaucratic, academic, and parliamentary politics. Here we can usually watch things happening with a specificity not accorded us in sex or science. Though early in their careers Snow's heroes dream of power in the abstract, their author is not really interested in power *qua* power. He does not, through symbols or a vast conspectus, give heroic character to natural, social, or industrial forces as Zola did in *Germinal* or Dos Passos in *U.S.A.* We do not see any charismatic leaders—Hitler, de Gaulle, Churchill, Roosevelt—directing or riding historic forces. We do not meet the masses to whom these men made their empowering appeal. We do not visit Lord Lufkin's factories or drop in at a rally of Roger Quaife's constituents. In *The Masters*, we get the impression that the thirteen fellows outnumber the students.

In one respect Snow is a naturalist. Each individual seems to him endowed with an unchangeable temperament which he must manage as best he can. There is no point in expecting him to be different from what he is. When Snow—or Lewis Eliot—accepts a person, he accepts him totally. It does not

[43]

matter to his friendship that Roy Calvert is a Nazi sympathizer or Ann Simon a Communist. It would not have mattered if the trial had proved George Passant to be intentionally dishonest. This principle fails to work only with Sheila, about whom Lewis complains so bitterly, but that is because he is bound to her by a temperamental need of his own that he cannot control and that he finds an intolerable burden.

Snow's novels are popular partly because his psychology is a classically humoral one. The Norse scholar Gay is happy and productive all his long life because it is in his sanguine nature to be so. Despite a happy marriage and success in the war, Nightingale misbehaves with the same bilious malice in *The Affair* as in *The Masters*. Roy Calvert is doomed by ineradicable and unsatisfiable yearnings that are at the very root of his melancholic being.

When Lewis does judge those close to him, it is always a particular practical judgment about how they will function in a given situation to achieve a given end. When a group of individuals is concerned, seeing how they will behave, how they will act and react to each other, takes on the fascination of a game of chess. Each man is limited by his nature to certain kinds of moves; but with enough pieces in play, and with some natures still unrevealed, all sorts of unpredictable combinations can occur.

Which side or issue wins does not count so much as the game itself and what it tells about the pieces or players. Those portions of the prose that are not straight dialogue consist largely of aphoristic comments on the rules of the game or a careful assessment of the contending forces within each man's psyche. There are a few added observations, characteristically general, of social changes in England in the past quarter-century.

Omitted in the later novels is any indication of how Lewis

Eliot himself is to be judged, or what price he has had to pay for his own success. He seems simply to have drifted upward into a position of influence and universal respect. And yet the psychic costs of success are amply evident elsewhere in the series. Perhaps Lewis Eliot's increasing blandness and self-satisfaction show what is happening, though here again we have the problem of separating Eliot from his creator. Snow has been made famous by his novels and his widely acclaimed public statements. He obviously delights in this public role, but it cannot have been entirely free from tensions, embarrassments, and moments of doubt. Neither for the joys or stresses and self-searchings has Snow found adequate equivalents in the later career of Lewis Eliot.

The new age of bureaucracy, where most things are done by committees, is ideal for the confrontations and character testings that Snow dramatizes so well. On the other hand, his interest in the individuals who confront each other is thoroughly traditional. Since he is not trying to say anything new psychologically, intellectually, or imaginatively, Snow is not driven to the technical extremism, the distortions in perspective, the "antihumanity" he condemns so roundly in most major twentieth-century writers. His fiction provides a comfortable compromise between new conditions and old forms. With it readers repelled by Beckett and Sarraute, Genet and Burroughs, can feel thoroughly at home. What a relief to have a narrator who is happily married, socially responsible, and reasonably confident about the future!

Abstractly and indirectly, Snow's world is a world of darkness and strangeness. Men are imprisoned in their own temperaments, are essentially alone when they suffer anguish of mind or body, and face a death of utter extinction. Concretely and immediately it is often a world of brotherhood and light. Men can learn to control or live with their temperaments. They are sustained by friendship, by love, by respect for institutions, by work, by shared ideas of justice and the common good. The sensible, unideological compromises of Snow's committee meetings are his model for that hoped-for understanding between the United States and Soviet Russia toward which so much of his public activity is directed. His private goal is different, though perhaps not incompatible. The nostalgic personal symbol in his novels is one of homecoming, of return with a wholly accepting and accepted companion to a small, warm—but very well lighted—room.

SELECTED BIBLIOGRAPHY

PRINCIPAL WORKS OF C. P. SNOW

Death under Sail. London, Heinemann, 1932; revised edition, 1939.

New Lives for Old. Published anonymously, London, Gollancz, 1933.

The Search. London, Gollancz, 1934; Indianapolis and New York, Bobbs-Merrill, 1935. Revised edition with preface, London, Macmillan, 1958; New York, Scribner's, 1958.

Strangers and Brothers. London, Faber & Faber, 1940; New York, Scribner's, 1960. Paperback edition: London, Penguin, 1962.

The Light and the Dark. London, Faber & Faber, 1947; New York, Macmillan, 1948.

Time of Hope. London, Faber & Faber, 1949; New York, Macmillan, 1950. Paperback edition: New York, Harper Torchbooks, 1961.

The Masters. London, Macmillan, 1951; New York, Macmillan, 1951. Paperback editions: London, Penguin, 1956; New York, Anchor (Doubleday), 1959.

The New Men. London, Macmillan, 1954; New York, Scribner's, 1954. Paperback editions: London, Penguin, 1959; New York, Scribner's, 1961.

Homecomings. London, Macmillan, 1956; (titled Homecoming) New York, Scribner's, 1956.

The Conscience of the Rich. London, Macmillan, 1958; New York, Scribner's, 1958. Paperback editions: New York, Scribner Library, 1960; London, Penguin, 1961.

The Two Cultures and The Scientific Revolution: The Rede Lecture. London, Cambridge University Press, 1959.

The Affair. London, Macmillan, 1960; New York, Scribner's, 1960. Paperback edition: London, Penguin, 1962.

Science and Government: Harvard University Godkin Lecture. Cambridge, Mass., Harvard University Press, 1961; London, Oxford University Press, 1961.

Appendix to Science and Government. Cambridge, Mass., Harvard University Press, 1962.

C. P. Snow: A Spectrum. Stanley Weintraub, ed. New York, Scribner's, 1963. (An anthology of selections from Snow's novels, speeches, and writings for periodicals.)

The Corridors of Power. London, Macmillan, 1964; New York, Scribner's, 1964.

"Afterthoughts by C. P. Snow," *Encounter*, XIV (February, 1960) 64–68. (A reply to the series of articles "The Two Cultures: A Discussion of C. P. Snow's Views.")

Bergonzi, Bernard. "The World of Lewis Eliot," *Twentieth Century*, CLXVII (February, 1960) 214–25.

Cooper, William. C. P. Snow. Writers and Their Work, Number 115. London and New York, Longmans, Green & Co., 1959.

Cornelius, David K., and Edwin St. Vincent, eds. Cultures in Conflict: Perspectives on the Snow-Leavis Controversy. Chicago, Scott, Foresman and Co., 1964.

Fison, Peter. "A Reply to Bernard Bergonzi's 'World of Lewis Eliot,'" *Twentieth Century*, CLXVII (June, 1960), 568–71.

Johnson, Pamela Hansford. "Three Novelists and the Drawing of Character (C. P. Snow, Joyce Cary and Ivy Compton-Burnett)," *Essays and Studies*, 1950, vol. 3 of the new series.

Karl, Frederick. C. P. Snow: The Politics of Conscience. Carbondale, Southern Illinois University Press, 1963.

Kermode, Frank. "Beckett, Snow and Pure Poverty," in Puzzles and Epiphanies. London, Routledge, 1962, pp. 155–63.

Leavis, F. R. "The Significance of C. P. Snow," *Spectator*, CCVIII (March 16, 1962), 297–303. Reprinted in Two Cultures? The Significance of C. P. Snow. With a preface by F. R. Leavis and "Sir Charles Snow's Rede Lecture" by Michael Yudkin. New York, Pantheon Books, 1963.

Muggeridge, Malcolm, and C. P. Snow. "Appointment with C. P. Snow" (excerpt from a television dialogue between Muggeridge and Snow), *Encounter*, XVIII (February, 1962), 90–93.

Nott, Kathleen. "The Type to Which the Whole Creation Moves?" *Encounter*, XVIII (February, 1962), 87–88, 94–97.

Thale, Jerome. C. P. Snow. Edinburgh and London, Oliver and Boyd, 1964. (Contains bibliography of writings by and about Snow.)

"The Two Cultures: A Discussion of C. P. Snow's Views," *Encounter*, XIII (August, 1959), 67–73; (September, 1959), 61–64; XIV (January, 1960), 72–73.

Trilling, Lionel. "The Novel Alive or Dead," in A Gathering of Fugitives. Boston, Beacon Press, 1956.

────── "Science, Literature and Culture: A Comment on the Leavis-Snow Controversy," *Commentary* (June, 1962), 461–77.